CRAYOLA
DIWALI
COLORS

MARI SCHUH

LERNER PUBLICATIONS ◆ MINNEAPOLIS

TO THE MARTIN COUNTY LIBRARY

Special thanks to content consultant Dr. Radha Balasubramanian, Professor of Russian and Director of Global Studies, Modern Languages & Literatures, University of Nebraska-Lincoln

Official Licensed Product
Lerner Publications Company
A division of Lerner Publishing Group, Inc.
241 First Avenue North
Minneapolis, MN 55401 USA

For reading levels and more information, look up this title at www.lernerbooks.com.

Main body text set in Billy Infant Regular 24/30.
Typeface provided by SparkyType.

Library of Congress Cataloging-in-Publication Data

Names: Schuh, Mari C., 1975- author.
Title: Crayola® Diwali colors / Mari Schuh.
Other titles: Diwali colors
Description: Minneapolis : Lerner Publications, 2018. | Series: Crayola® holiday colors | Includes bibliographical references and index. | Audience: Age 4-9. | Audience: K to grade 3. | Description based on print version record and CIP data provided by publisher; resource not viewed.
Identifiers: LCCN 2017044251 (print) | LCCN 2017056983 (ebook) | ISBN 9781541512443 (eb pdf) | ISBN 9781541510906 (lb : alk. paper) | ISBN 9781541527478 (pb : alk. paper)
Subjects: LCSH: Diwali—Juvenile literature. | Colors—Juvenile literature.
Classification: LCC BL1239.82.D58 (ebook) | LCC BL1239.82.D58 S35 2018 (print) | DDC 394.265/45—dc23

LC record available at https://lccn.loc.gov/2017044251

Manufactured in the United States of America
1-43974-33988-12/5/2017

TABLE OF CONTENTS

WHAT IS DIWALI?

Families gather, and oil lamps glow. People prepare colorful sweets, buy fireworks, and get their new clothes ready to wear.

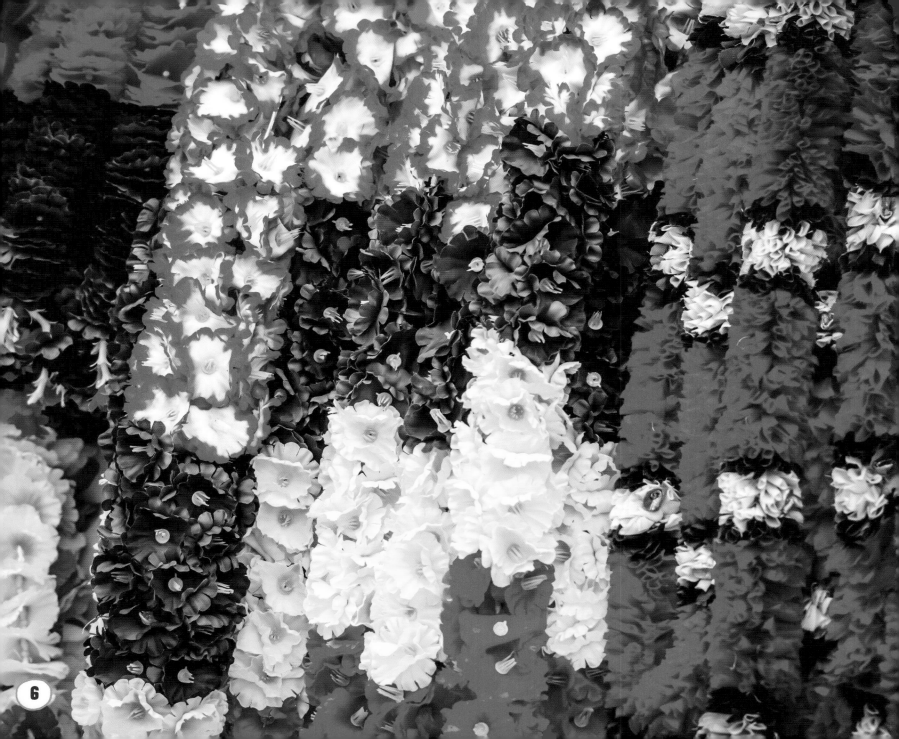

People in India and around the world celebrate Diwali in fall.

Diwali is the biggest and brightest holiday in India. People clean their homes and decorate.

FESTIVAL OF LIGHTS

Diwali is a Hindu holiday. It is celebrated on the darkest night of the new moon.

Lamps and lanterns shine **GREEN**, **PINK**, **YELLOW**, and **BLUE**.

9

During Diwali, the **GOLDEN** glow of clay lamps fills the home.

These small clay lamps are called *diyas*.

Bright sparklers and noisy fireworks light up the night.

This family celebrates Diwali with sparklers.

Rangoli is made with colored powder, chalk, sand, and flower petals.

COLORFUL TRADITIONS

COLORFUL patterns on the floor welcome guests. This art is called *rangoli.*

PINK, ORANGE, GREEN, and YELLOW!

Traditional clothing worn on Diwali is bright and bold.

There are many ways to wear color!
Women wear **REDDISH-BROWN** henna on their hands and feet.

Henna marks good fortune and success.

During Diwali, people pray for wealth and good fortune.

They offer coins, rice, spices, and sweets.

GOLD and **SILVER** goods sparkle in the market.

Buyers hope these items will bring riches and good luck for the next year.

YELLOW, ORANGE, and GREEN.

People fill their plates with color during Diwali.

They share sweets with
family and friends.

A TIME OF JOY

Gifts are a way to show love and good wishes during Diwali.

Diwali is a time to pray and give thanks.

Diwali is filled with color and joy!

COPY AND COLOR!

Diwali is a colorful holiday for the whole family! Here are some of the Crayola® crayon colors used in this book. What colors will you use to celebrate? Copy these pages, and color the symbols of Diwali.

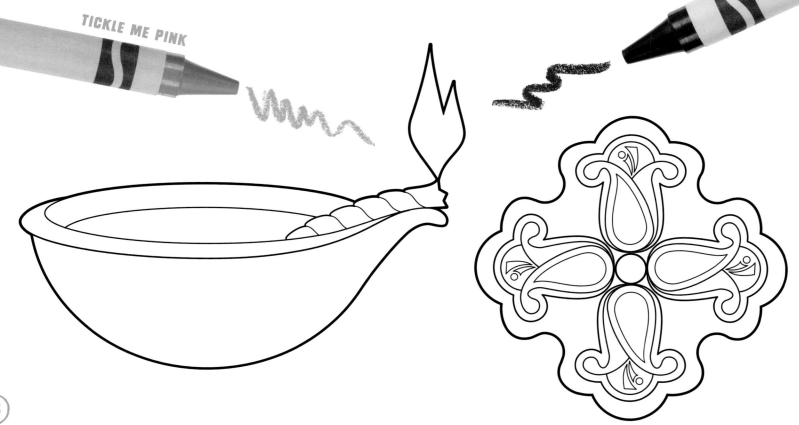

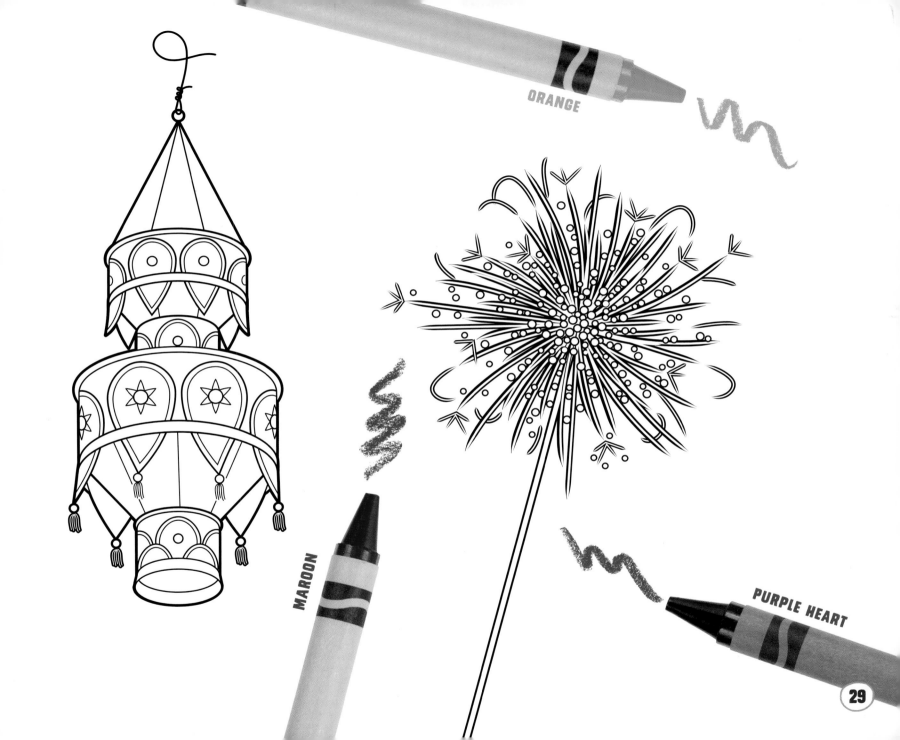

ORANGE

MAROON

PURPLE HEART

GLOSSARY

fireworks: devices that are loud and colorful when they are burned or exploded. Fireworks are used at celebrations.

henna: a reddish-brown dye. Henna is made from the leaves of the henna plant.

Hindu: a religion practiced mainly in India

lanterns: lights with frames around them

rangoli: art that uses materials such as colored powder, chalk, sand, and flower petals to make patterns on a floor

riches: lots of money

sparklers: flammable sticks that people hold in their hands and that let off bright sparks as they burn

traditional: a way of doing something that has been passed on through time

TO LEARN MORE

BOOKS

Koestler-Grack, Rachel. *Diwali*. Minneapolis: Bellwether, 2017. Read about the history of Diwali and why it is an important holiday.

Murray, Julie. *Diwali*. Minneapolis: Abdo Kids, 2018. Discover the festivities and activities that happen during Diwali.

Sebra, Richard. *It's Diwali!* Minneapolis: Lerner Publications, 2017. Learn more about the many celebrations of Diwali.

WEBSITES

Diwali Crafts
https://www.activityvillage.co.uk/diwali-crafts
Celebrate Diwali by making several Diwali crafts.

Diwali Light
http://www.crayola.com/crafts/diwali-light-craft/
Learn how to make a pretend light using colorful tissue paper.

National Geographic Kids: Diwali
http://kids.nationalgeographic.com/explore/diwali/
Read about Diwali and how this important holiday got its name.

INDEX

PHOTO ACKNOWLEDGMENTS

The images in this book are used with the permission of: Texture ART/Alamy Stock Photo, p. 1; vtaurus/Shutterstock.com, pp. 2, 3, 30, 31, 32 (red pattern); India Picture/Shutterstock.com, pp. 4, 13, 26; Indianstockimages/Shutterstock.com, p. 5 (top left); Milind Arvind Ketkar/Shutterstock.com, p. 5 (top right); Jasni/Shutterstock.com, p. 5 (bottom left); Pikoso.kz/Shutterstock.com, p. 5 (bottom right); MagicColors/Getty Images, p. 6; Shyamalamuralinath/Shutterstock.com, p. 7; TheFinalMiracle/Shutterstock.com, pp. 8-9; Kulpreet_Photography/Getty Images, pp. 10-11; ImagesBazaar/Getty Images, p. 12; indianeye/Getty Images, p. 14; Dinendra Haria/Alamy Stock Photo, pp. 16, 17; © Josh Rodriguez/flickr.com (CC BY-SA 2.0), pp. 18-19; Intellistudies/Shutterstock.com, pp. 20-21; Prabhat Kumar Verma/ZUMA Press, Inc./Alamy Stock Photo, p. 23; Arisha Ray Singh/Shutterstock.com, p. 25; NARINDER NANU/AFP/Getty Images), p. 27; © Laura Westlund/Independent Picture Service, pp. 28, 29 (illustrations).

Cover: Kinsei/Shutterstock.com (flowers); © Josh Rodriguez/flickr.com (CC BY-SA 2.0) (hands); Wan Fahmy Redzuan/Shutterstock.com (kolam drawing).